Sydney Clair's
SEASON OF CHANGE

A FRIENDSHIP STORY

PAM DAVIS

Authentic

COLORADO SPRINGS • MILTON KEYNES • HYDERABAD

Authentic Publishing
We welcome your questions and comments.

USA   1820 Jet Stream Drive, Colorado Springs, CO 80921 www.authenticbooks.com
UK   9 Holdom Avenue, Bletchley, Milton Keynes, Bucks, MK1 1QR
       www.authenticmedia.co.uk
India Logos Bhavan, Medchal Road, Jeedimetla Village, Secunderabad 500 055, A.P.

Sydney Clair's Season of Change: A Friendship Story
ISBN-13: 978-1-934068-50-2
ISBN-10: 1-934068-50-0

Scripture quotations are taken from the authorized King James Version. Public domain.

Photo credits: The photographs that appear in the book are courtesy of Austin Library.
Author photo: Cliff Ranson, www.ransonphotography.com.
Images: © 2007 iStockphoto.com, and © 2007 JupiterImages Corporation

Illustrations: Monica Bucanelli
Cover/Interior design: Julia Ryan | www.DesignByJulia.com
Editorial team: Kathy Buchanan, Reagen Reed, Megan Kassebaum

Printed in the United States of America

CONTENTS

*To Ann Hawkins, my mother and my
first encounter with a girl in grace.*

Welcome from the Author

Dear friends,

I am so pleased you are joining me as we journey through lives of girls in grace.

A Girl 'n Grace is a girl in whom the person of grace, Jesus Christ, lives. You'll notice there's a missing "I" and an apostrophe in its place. The Bible teaches that in order to live in a relationship with God one must surrender her life to Jesus. No longer do I live but rather it is Christ who lives in me as I live by faith in the Son of God (Galatians 2:20). A Girl 'n Grace is a girl who has surrendered her self-centered desires to the desires of Christ. In doing so, she discovers strength, satisfaction, and significance, which elevates her self-esteem and honors God.

Let this book aid you in discovering the desires of Jesus Christ and may you, like these characters, proclaim, "I can through Christ."®

In his embrace,
Pam Davis
(ACTS 20:24)

Sydney Clair Wilcox is a determined,
curious ten-year-old trying to keep up with
all the changes around her. The year is 1965
and Penny, her beloved big sister, is moving
away to college. In the middle of the civil rights,
women's rights, and environmental movements,
Sydney Clair's world is changing. Discover how her
heart is made ready for the next season of her
life and how she prepares for a fragrant
friendship that blooms.

Things have changed a great deal since the 1960s when Sydney Clair
grew up. Things that were popular then, like getting a new pair of
gloves to wear for a special party, seem old-fashioned now. The
language that was used has changed as well. Both white and
black people would refer to African-Americans as "Negroes"
or "Coloreds." Since that time the American culture no
longer considers those words acceptable. But because
this book is written from a ten-year-old's perspective
living in the 60s, we chose to include those
words in Sydney Clair's story.

Girls 'n Grace Place

Girls 'n Grace Place is a fun website where you can interact with the Girls 'n Grace characters. You can . . .

join the free Reader's Club to take a quiz and win a prize! These heart-shaped icons in the book tell you there's a quiz question on the website.

participate with the Girls 'n Grace doll characters through a virtual experience and enjoy a wide range of activities: fashion, reader's club, travel, cooking, decorating, art, education, creating your own Girls 'n Grace magazine, and much more!

Visit the Girls 'n Grace characters at www.girlsngrace.com.

CHAPTER 1

Changes

It's going to be a bad day, Sydney Clair thought to herself. She snuggled deeper under the covers. Maybe if she stayed in bed all day, nothing would change. Her sister wouldn't leave. She'd stay right here with the rest of the family, the way things had always been.

But she could already hear Penny moving about the room they shared, packing last-minute items and singing to herself. Sydney Clair pulled the pillow over her head.

It sounded like she was taking everything.

"Not the dancing clowns!" Sydney Clair removed the pillow when she heard the music box.

Penny smiled. "Don't worry. I'm not taking the dancing clowns."

Sydney Clair thought her sister was the prettiest girl ever. She blinked back tears, but Penny still saw them.

"I'm only a twenty-minute bus ride away, Clair-Bear. You can come visit anytime."

Clair-Bear. It was a nickname her sister had given her when she was just a baby. She'd loved it when she was little.

Sydney wasn't a very common name amongst her friends' Susies, Vickys, and Lucys. Mother had named her Sydney in honor of her grandfather who passed away shortly before Sydney Clair was born. Now Sydney Clair appreciated the name more—and liked the uniqueness of it—but "Clair-Bear" still had a special place in her heart. Though, with Penny leaving, who would call her that now? And who would braid her hair for school? Who could she talk to about what was happening in her favorite book series? Who would walk down to the Dairy Queen with her for Dilly Bars?

Who would be her sister?

♡ ♡ ♡

The family's Plymouth station wagon meandered its way onto the University of Texas campus. Sydney Clair could tell Penny was practically bursting with excitement. She stared out the window, pointing to every statue and building on campus. "That's Hogg Memorial Auditorium. That's Austin Tower. You can see the whole campus from the top of it."

Sydney Clair didn't even pretend to be interested. But her dad slowed down the car and stretched to see the Tower. "Can you read the inscription?" he asked.

"And ye shall know the truth and the truth shall make you free," quoted Penny. "Isn't that a Bible verse?"

Mother nodded. "John 8:32, I believe."

"Ding, ding, ding," Mr. Wilcox chimed. "Your mother wins the prize."

"And what might that prize be?" Mother asked teasingly.

"Uh . . . I'll make dinner tonight," Mr. Wilcox said.

"That means we're having peanut butter and jelly," Sydney Clair interjected from the back seat.

"Or corn chips and soda pop," said her mother, laughing.

Mr. Wilcox pretended to pout. "You have no confidence at all in my cooking abilities."

"I'm just remembering when you made me that birthday cake while we were dating."

"Uh, oh. Don't bring that up . . . " Mr. Wilcox said.

"What was wrong with it, Mother?" Penny asked.

Mother turned her head to look at the girls. "He decided to frost it before he put it in the oven." She began to laugh. "When he took it out, the whole top was charred black."

"I didn't know you were supposed to bake the cake first and *then* decorate it," Dad said with a grin on his face. "And, bless her heart, your mother ate it anyway."

"What you lacked in culinary skills, you more than made up for in charm," Mother told him.

"I'm voting that Mother keeps her job of doing the cooking," said Sydney Clair.

Sydney Clair tried to imagine her mother and dad before they were married. She knew they must have laughed a lot— because even now they were always joking about something.

Her dad pulled into a parking spot and shut off the engine in front of Penny's dormitory.

"Here we are," said Mr. Wilcox. "Bradshaw Hall."

"Isn't it beautiful?" said Penny.

"It's very stately," Mrs. Wilcox agreed, opening her car door.

All Sydney Clair saw was a boring brick building. She stepped out into the hot, dusty Austin summer, already feeling the start of sweat on her temples. Not only was her sister abandoning her to go to college, but she'd have to spend the next few hours carrying boxes up and down stairs.

"What's going on over there?" Mrs. Wilcox asked. Sydney Clair looked in the direction she was pointing toward and saw a swarm of college students marching around in a circle waving signs. Some seemed to have relinquished themselves to the heat and sat lounging in small circles on the grass.

"They're protesting bleached toilet paper," said Penny. "Leah told me all about it. Companies whiten toilet paper with chemicals that can ruin our environment. It needs to be stopped."

Leah was Penny's best friend and an expert in everything.

"We should get started," Mr. Wilcox said. He lifted a large box out of the back of the station wagon.

Sydney Clair kept watching the protesters. A young man, whose hair hung down to his waist and wore a colorful headband, seemed to be in charge. He shouted from the steps of a building, waving his sign high in the air. Like the others, he wore frayed blue jeans, and his feet were bare. "The land has taken good care of us—we need to take good care of it!"

The other protesters shouted back in agreement. "Right on, man!" "That's right!" "Protect our planet!"

Sydney Clair's dad broke into her thoughts. "If I'd have worn my hair like that, your grandmother would've never let me out of the house."

♡ ♡ ♡

Sydney Clair lost count of the number of times she climbed the three flights of stairs to Penny's new room.

She still didn't understand why Penny was so excited about college. The room they shared at home was twice the size of this one. She felt her eyes moisten thinking about sleeping in the room all by herself.

As Sydney Clair reached the third floor for the umpteenth time, Penny's squealing voice caught her attention. "It's so great to finally meet you!"

Sydney Clair turned into Penny's dorm room and plopped down the avocado green beanbag she'd been carrying. A red-haired girl. who wore a peasant blouse and a denim skirt, sat cross-legged on the bed next to her sister.

"Sydney Clair, this is Moonbeam," Penny said. "My roommate."

Sydney Clair quickly shoved aside the thought that *she* used to be Penny's roommate. "Hi," she mustered. She wondered what Moonbeam's parents had named her brothers and sisters. *Star? Planet? Galaxy? Were they astronomers?*

"Peace," Moonbeam said, holding up two fingers in a V-shape.

"What are your sisters and brothers named?" asked Sydney Clair.

"What kind of question is that?" Penny said.

"It's cool," said Moonbeam. "I have two brothers, named Jack and Harry."

"Those names are pretty normal," said Sydney Clair. "Why isn't yours?"

Penny glared at her. "Sydney Clair!" she scolded.

"No sweat. Little Daisy here is curious," said Moonbeam. "My parents named me Shirley. But I chose Moonbeam. It seemed to fit my personality better—y'know, who I *really* am. I shine in the midst of dark ideas."

Penny nodded in agreement, but Sydney Clair thought it was just plain weird. Why was Moonbeam calling her Daisy? She liked the names Shirley and Sydney Clair better but thought it best not to say.

"You have to listen to this record," Moonbeam was saying. "Have you heard of Jefferson Airplane?"

"No, but I really like the Beatles. And Peter, Paul, and Mary," Penny said.

Moonbeam nodded approvingly. "Their song 'Blowin' in the Wind' is far-out."

Sydney Clair noticed a guitar case in the corner. "Do you play the guitar?"

"I'm learning," said Moonbeam. "Maybe someday it'll be the group Peter, Paul, and Moonbeam."

Sydney Clair didn't think so, but she kept her mouth shut.

Another girl burst into the room. "Guess what, Moonbeam! We have a colored girl on the floor."

Moonbeam quickly introduced Sydney Clair and Penny to Beth. "What room is she in?"

"Two doors down."

"Didn't the University of Texas open up to colored students several years ago?" asked Penny.

"Sure," said Beth. "But this is my third year here, and I've never lived on the same floor as one before."

Sydney Clair wondered what was taking her parents so long. She didn't really like college life. But she knew she felt bad for the colored girl living two doors down. She hadn't been exposed to a lot of colored people in her life. There weren't any Negro families in her neighborhood. Only a handful of colored kids went to her school and they pretty much stuck to themselves.

"Well, I don't have a problem with it," stated Moonbeam.

"I do. And my mother certainly will when she finds out. She's from Alabama, and things are different there," said Beth. She started talking about some town named Birmingham and how the town residents set buses on fire that Freedom Riders were riding.

Sydney Clair wondered who Freedom Riders were. The whole thing sounded scary.

A knocking sound came from the hallway.

"Come in," called Moonbeam.

A petite colored girl swung open the door. She wore a white blouse and plaid skirt. "Sorry to bother you. Can you tell me how to get to the library?"

Moonbeam started giving directions, but Sydney Clair noticed that Beth turned away and stared out the window.

♡ ♡ ♡

Outside her car window, Sydney Clair watched the pink sunset fade into the Texas plain. It had been a long day, and she was tired.

"I hear some larger companies are coming into town. There will be some good-paying jobs opening up," Mother was telling Dad.

Mother often talked about "larger corporations" these days, but Dad never seemed as interested. "And all those good-paying jobs will require a suit and tie," he said.

"I think you'd look very handsome in a tie," Mrs. Wilcox said.

Sydney Clair was still thinking about the university they'd just left. The whole place seemed crazy and loud and chaotic. Even as they'd pulled out of the parking lot, girls wearing flower wreaths in their hair waved signs saying, "Bring our GIs home!" She remembered the young man with the long hair. Yep . . . college was a far cry from the white picket fences of their quiet neighborhood, where walking to the Piggly Wiggly for candy was enough for excitement.

"Don't you like the name Shirley better than Moonbeam?" she asked her parents.

Mr. Wilcox chuckled as he drove. "College students have their own way of doing things."

"Especially in this day and age," said Mrs. Wilcox. "I hope Penny does okay there."

"She'll be fine." Mr. Wilcox patted his wife's hand. "We've raised her well."

"Do you think she'll change?" Sydney Clair wondered aloud.

"In some ways," her dad said. "She's growing up. She'll be learning new things, meeting new people."

"I mean *really* change. Will she still be *our* Penny?"

"She'll always be our Penny," her mother said.

♡ ♡ ♡

Sydney Clair was still missing her sister as she and her mother washed the dishes that evening. The sounds of *The Dick Van Dyke Show* wafted in from the next room where her dad sat in his easy chair with the newspaper. ♡ Her mother had made Sydney Clair's favorite dinner—roast beef with mashed potatoes—but it hadn't cheered her up much. She kept thinking of Penny at college.

"There's only three of everything," she said. "Three plates, three forks." She handed her mother a sudsy glass to rinse. "Three glasses."

"I guess things change," Mrs. Wilcox said. "They'll always

change. Someday you'll go off to college and move away from home."

"Maybe I'll just move into the playhouse," said Sydney Clair. Her dad had built her a new playhouse over the summer. It was better than any playhouse she'd ever seen, and her friends Vicky and Ann had agreed. It  had shutters that opened and closed, a little kitchen with a sink that held water, and even electricity for the light that hung over the table. Mrs. Wilcox often brought cookies or snacks to Sydney Clair and her friends, who regularly hosted tea parties from the playhouse. Inside the playhouse or out on the lawn in front—it didn't matter. Mrs. Wilcox would often say, "You need to eat more than just tea and crumpets," which were usually Kool-Aid and corn chips. But with Sydney Clair's imagination, they were never just tea and crumpets. They were exotic concoctions from far off lands. Sydney Clair cherished her playhouse. *Because it never changed,* she thought.

Her mother chuckled. "Someday you'll even outgrow the playhouse."

Sydney Clair couldn't imagine that.

Mr. Wilcox walked into the kitchen, carrying the newspaper. "Did you see this article, dear?" He handed Mrs. Wilcox the newspaper, and they started talking about some race riots that had taken place in California.

"Do you know there's a colored girl that lives on Penny's floor?" Sydney Clair said.

Mrs. Wilcox nodded. "Yes, and I hope your sister will make sure she feels welcome."

"Knowing Penny, she'll do just that," said Mr. Wilcox. "Can I help you finish the dishes?"

"As always, your timing is perfect," said Mother. "We just finished."

"And I missed it," Mr. Wilcox feigned disappointment.

"Someday we'll have to get one of those new automatic dishwashers they have out now. We'd be done doing dishes in no time," said Sydney Clair.

"I thought *you* were my automatic dishwasher, Sydney Clair." Her mother smiled.

"I think she might need a tune-up," Dad said. "She's slowing down a little."

"Maybe she needs some chocolate cake to get her going again," Mother suggested.

Sydney Clair's spirits lifted a bit. "We have chocolate cake for dessert?"

"We do," Mrs. Wilcox said, her eyes twinkling. "And because I love you so much, I baked the cake before I frosted it."

"Wow, what an interesting idea," said Sydney Clair.

"I can tell when I'm being made fun of," Mr. Wilcox said. "But I'm still sticking around for chocolate cake."

♡ ♡ ♡

Sydney Clair chewed on the end of her pencil while she stared at her calendar. Bo, the family's golden retriever, brushed past Sydney Clair's bare legs and curled up on a rug in the middle of the floor. Every day, Sydney Clair would write either "good day" or "bad day" to describe how the day had gone. All day, she'd planned that this would be a "bad day." She mindlessly scratched behind Bo's ears.

"Boy, I'm really going to miss Penny," she said. Penny's bare bed, now stripped of its pink sheets, made the room look so empty.

Bo looked up at her with big brown eyes, as if he understood Sydney Clair's sadness.

"At least I still have you to keep me company," Sydney Clair told him.

Bo answered by putting his head on his paws.

Sydney Clair penciled "bad day" on the calendar. But then she thought about joking around with her parents, having chocolate cake, and talking to her mom about going shopping for school. *I guess it wasn't all bad*, she thought. Sydney Clair jotted "mostly" in front of "bad day."

"What do you think, Bo?" she asked.

The dog perked up and seemed to smile back in agreement.

CHAPTER 2

Friends

"We can put the tea set here," said Vicky. "But be careful. It's breakable."

Sydney Clair started arranging the teapot and cups on the table inside her playhouse.

Vicky continued, "I'll be the duchess of Madagascar, and you can be my duchess friends. We'll use these as our crumpets." She put out the peanut butter cookies Sydney Clair's mother had made that morning.

"What are crumpets again?" asked Sydney Clair.

"English treats, of course. Only the best for the duchesses."

Ann, who was scratching Bo behind the ears, perked up. "Groovy! And the duchess of Madagascar can get poisoned by the crumpet, and then Sydney Clair and I can investigate to see who was out to murder her!"

Vicky impatiently stirred inside the empty cup. "That's not what I was planning. Why can't we just have a nice tea for once?"

"Because that's boring!" said Ann.

"Well, you haven't met our minstrels yet," said Vicky.

"What are minstrels?" asked Sydney Clair.

"Entertainment for royalty. They're *very* talented."

"Are you having minstrels at your birthday party, Victoria?" asked Ann, with a little bit of sarcasm.

Vicky's face burst into a grin. She loved talking about her birthday party. "No, but we are going to have pony rides. My dad called the place last night. And they're going to bring a pony right into our backyard!"

"What kind of cake is your mother making?" asked Sydney Clair.

"She's not! The Cisco Bakery is making it. It's going to be huge, with lots and lots of fluffy pink icing. And it'll say 'Happy Birthday, Vicky!' in big pink letters."

"I can't wait," said Sydney Clair. She'd been looking forward to Vicky's birthday party ever since Vicky had started talking about it months ago.

"And we'll have a whole table of snacks and desserts and a big glass punch bowl with real glasses! And my mother even hired a band, so there will be dancing, too! You have to dress up and wear a hat. Mother says everyone dresses up for nice parties like this."

Ann, clearly bored of the conversation, reached for a "crumpet."

"Sounds lovely," she said in a fake accent. She took a big bite of the cookie. Her eyes widened and she collapsed onto the floor.

"Ann?" said Sydney Clair.

"Somebody . . . has plotted . . . to kill me," Ann gasped in her fake accent. "You must . . . find them." She rolled over onto her back, flailing back her arms and letting her tongue loll out of her mouth.

Sydney Clair giggled. Ann reminded her of the way Bo looked last night. Vicky, less amused, rolled her eyes.

A knock sounded at the door.

"It's our first suspect," said Sydney Clair. She flung the door open.

Her mother stood on the other side. "Sydney Clair, I don't want to interrupt your fun, but I need to go to the library for my shift. Are you ready to go?"

Bo dashed out of the playhouse like a prisoner given a pardon.

"Yes, ma'am," Sydney Clair said. She turned to her friends. "Sorry, girls. We'll have to finish this later."

Ann picked herself up off the floor.

"Next time, maybe we can have a civil tea," muttered Vicky.

"Well, Victoria, don't bring those minstrels then," said Ann, then lowered her voice. "I think they're the ones who poisoned the crumpets."

Although a little disappointed to leave her friends, Sydney Clair didn't mind going to the library. Her mother had started a part-time job there several months ago, and Sydney Clair always loved to pick out books and read while her mother worked. Her favorite spot was an old couch set up in a back room where hardly anyone ever went. Mother said it was the reference room. It smelled like old, dusty books, and Sydney Clair thought that's what smart people's houses must smell like.

She picked out a book from her favorite series, Little House on the Prairie, and headed back to the reference room. To her dismay, she saw a little girl already curled up on the couch—a little colored girl Sydney Clair guessed to be about her own age.

The girl looked up and saw Sydney Clair looking at her. The two watched each other silently for a few seconds before the little colored girl spoke. "Why are you staring at me? I didn't steal nothin'!"

Sydney Clair was surprised by the outburst. "I didn't say you stole anything. It's just that you're sitting where I usually sit."

"I'll move." The girl started to slide off the couch.

"No, you don't have to move," Sydney Clair said. "I just . . . wasn't expecting anyone to be here."

"Yeah. And there ain't many colored girls in the library, right?"

"Not usually," Sydney Clair said, still looking at the girl. She'd never been this close to a Negro before, and she really didn't know what to do. Was it okay that they talk? What was she supposed to say?

The girl's hard features softened a bit. "I'm sorry I snapped at you. Usually people only talk to me when they think I swiped something. Like yesterday this lady said I took her purse. But I didn't."

"I believe you," Sydney Clair said. "Did she ever find it?"

"My momma found it in the bathroom. But the lady still said I hid it there. I think she was just embarrassed," the girl said.

"But it's still not fair," Sydney Clair said. "By the way, my name's Sydney Clair."

A smile broke out on the girl's face. "I'm Patrice. My momma is a cleaning lady here, so I come in to read while she works."

"My mother works here, too. At the front desk. What are you reading?"

The girl held up her book, *On the Banks of Plum Creek.*

"I'm reading the same series!" Sydney Clair held up her own book, *The Long Winter.* "I've read that one already," she said as she pointed to Patrice's book. "It's really good."

Patrice smiled. "And I read *that* one before. It's good, too. I think it's my favorite in the whole series."

Sydney Clair noticed the curls of Patrice's hair, her chocolate-colored skin, and her pretty, brown eyes. Patrice wore her hair back in a headband that matched her dress. Sydney Clair wished she had a matching ensemble like that.

"I just got to the part where Almanzo and Cap go out into the blizzard to get help," said Sydney Clair. "I'm worried they're not going to make it back. And I really like Almanzo."

Patrice nodded. "I can tell you what happens if you want."

"Yes!"

"Well, they run into—" Patrice began, but Sydney Clair interrupted.

"No, stop. Don't tell me!" Sydney Clair really wanted to know what would happen, but it would be more fun to read it on her own.

"Alright. . . ."

But Sydney Clair was worried, so maybe she would find out if everything would end okay. "Well, just tell me how it ends."

"Okay, it—" Patrice started again.

"No, wait. Don't!"

Both girls started to laugh at Sydney Clair's indecisiveness.

"You're funny," said Patrice.

"It's kind of like Christmas," said Sydney Clair. "You want to know what you're going to get, but you also don't want to ruin the surprise of opening up your present on Christmas Day."

"Do you ever ask your momma for hints?" asked Patrice.

"Every year," said Sydney Clair. "But she never tells me!"

"She must be talking to my momma! She never tells me nothin' either!"

The girls' giggling was broken into by a loud "Shhhh!"

A large woman approached them, looking cross. "You girls need to be quiet. This is a library," she scolded.

"Sorry," Sydney Clair said.

The woman looked from Sydney Clair to Patrice and back to Sydney Clair again. "Does your mother know where you are?"

Sydney Clair nodded. She knew that the woman meant "Does your mother know who you're with?" And the thought crossed her mind that maybe she was doing something wrong.

The woman gave them one more stern look and shuffled away.

Sydney Clair suddenly felt the urge to get away from the scrutiny of this woman—of anyone who was looking at her strangely. She noticed her legs were sticking together and the room was growing hotter as the afternoon sunshine poured in the window. "Do you want to go get some ice cream?" she asked Patrice.

"Mmm . . . ice cream sounds really good," said Patrice.

"There's a man with an ice cream cart at the end of the block. Let's go ask our mothers if we can go."

The girls tried to contain their excitement as they hurried through the library to find their mothers. They found Mrs. Wilcox first.

"Mother, can Patrice and I get some ice cream?" Sydney Clair pleaded from her tip toes.

"Oh, good. I see you met Patrice," she said. "I've really enjoyed getting to know your mother, Patrice."

"You must be Mrs. Wilcox," said Patrice. "My mother talks about you at home."

A tall colored woman approached them. "Patrice, keep your voice down," she warned. She flashed a bright smile and gave the girls a wink. Sydney Clair liked her right away.

"Hi, Dorthea," Mrs. Wilcox said. "The girls want to go out for ice cream."

"Is that okay, Momma?" Patrice asked.

Dorthea straightened the kerchief wrapped around her head. "I don't see why not." She fished out some change from her apron pocket and handed it to Patrice. "Now be off with you. I need to get back to work."

♡ ♡ ♡

The heat from the sun was nearly unbearable as Patrice and Sydney Clair made their way down the sidewalk.

"It's hot enough to bake biscuits on the porch," said Patrice. Sydney Clair agreed.

"I think I'm going to mark this day as a good day," Sydney Clair decided out loud.

"What's that mean?" asked Patrice.

"Every day I write down on my calendar if it was a good day or a bad day," Sidney Clair explained.

"That's a neat idea," Patrice said. "I think I'll start doing that."

"What are you going to put down for today?" asked Sydney Clair. She couldn't help but notice Patrice's worn shoes. They had holes in the tops and looked about a hundred years old.

Patrice nodded to the ice cream cart they were closing in on. "Depends how good the strawberry ice cream is."

"Strawberry's my favorite, too," said Sydney Clair. "And, trust me, Henry has great strawberry ice cream."

Henry, the ice cream man, recognized Sydney Clair right away. She was a frequent customer. "Hello there, blondie," he said. "What can I get you today?"

"We'll take two strawberry cones."

"Sorry, I don't serve Negroes," Henry said curtly.

Sydney Clair was taken aback. "But . . . we both want ice cream."

"That's the way it is. Here you go." Henry handed Sydney Clair her cone without giving Patrice another glance, and then turned to another customer.

Sydney Clair numbly clutched her cone. She couldn't believe what Henry had said. Why wouldn't he give Patrice ice cream?

"We'll just share," she said to Patrice.

Patrice bit her lip.

The walk back to the library seemed to take twice as long. Patrice said she didn't want any of Sydney Clair's ice cream, although Sydney Clair offered several times.

"So I guess this means you're marking it a bad day today," Sydney Clair said.

Patrice shrugged. "If I let stuff like that decide, every day would be a bad day."

"Really? It doesn't make sense. I mean, you were going to pay for it. Why does it matter?"

"It's just the way it is," Patrice said, repeating what Henry had told them.

"Oh."

"I'm kind of used to it. We just moved into a new neighborhood a couple weeks ago—a white neighborhood. And people are trying to get us to leave because we're colored."

Sydney Clair's eyes widened. "They actually asked you to move?"

"Worse than that," Patrice said. "They put mean notes on our door. The second night we were there, someone threw a brick through our front window."

The two walked to the library steps in silence while Sydney Clair pondered this. She'd never heard of anything like that.

"I think it could even be a good day still," Patrice said as they climbed the stone stairs.

"Really?" Sydney Clair didn't understand. She knew if she'd been treated like that, it might be the worst day of her life.

"Yes. Because I made a new friend—one who also worried that Almanzo might not make it back safely."

Sydney Clair smiled. She was glad to be part of Patrice's good day.

♡ ♡ ♡

"Why wouldn't Henry give Patrice ice cream today?" Sydney Clair asked her mother on the way home.

"Some people don't believe colored people deserve to be treated as well as white people," her mother answered.

Sydney Clair stared out the bus window. Clouds had begun to cover the sky, giving some much-needed relief from the heat.

"Why? They're still people."

Mrs. Wilcox smiled. "I wish everyone could think like you do. It's a big issue in our country today. For years, colored people have organized marches and rallies all over the country to show that they deserve equal rights. Have you heard of Dr. Martin Luther King Jr.?"

Sydney Clair had heard the name, but she didn't know much about him.

Her mother continued. "A couple of years ago, 250,000 people marched in Washington, D.C., in support of equal rights for Negros. Dr. King gave a very powerful speech about what he thought the future should look like. He said he wanted a future where colored people and white people could enjoy the same privileges and coexist amiably."

Sydney Clair remembered what Beth had said about the buses in Birmingham. "Does he set things on fire?"

"No, he doesn't. He believes in peacefully making changes—not acting violently."

Sydney Clair remembered what Patrice had said about her front window. In many ways she and Patrice were so similar—they liked the same books and the same kind of ice cream—yet their lives were decidedly different. Her big concern these days was when her dad was going to put knobs on the cabinets in her playhouse. She didn't have to worry about someone trying to hurt her—or her family. "I feel bad for them," she murmured.

"You mean Patrice's family?"

Sydney Clair thought about the colored girl on Penny's floor at college and the way Beth turned her back on her. "I guess I mean Negroes in general."

Mother nodded. "In his speech, Dr. King said his dream was that his children would not be judged by the color of their skin but by the content of their character."

"I like that," said Sydney Clair. "What else did he say?"

"The other part I remember him saying was 'I have a dream that one day little black boys and black girls will be able to join hands with little white boys and white girls as sisters and brothers.'"

Sydney Clair decided if she ever met Dr. King, she'd probably really like him.

"Grandmother!"

Sydney Clair opened the door to a big, warm hug from her grandmother. Grandmother Wilcox came over for dinner about once a week.

"Let's get inside, child. It's hotter than the lake of fire out here!"

Sydney Clair helped Grandmother in while Mother apologized for Dad not being home yet. "Factory work can be so grueling. I'm hoping he starts to look for an office job soon."

Grandmother nodded, unconcerned. "I just happened to stop by the store on the way here and found these," she said, taking a small package out of her purse. Grandmother always brought a small gift for Sydney Clair when she came over.

Sydney Clair tore into the package. "The socks I wanted!" They were white with lacy cuffs. She'd wanted some for the first day of school. "Thank you, Grandmother!"

"You're welcome, dear."

Mr. Wilcox came home shortly, and Mother called everyone together for dinner. After Dad prayed over the meal, Grandmother turned to Sydney Clair. "So how was your day, Sydney Clair?"

"I met a new friend at the library," Sydney Clair said.

Grandmother nodded. "And what's her name?"

"Patrice. She's really nice, and she reads Little House on the Prairie books just like I do. But Henry, the ice cream guy, wouldn't serve her ice cream because she's a Negro."

Grandmother started to cough. "She's a *colored* girl!?"

"Yes, ma'am," Sydney Clair said. Grandmother was clearly bothered. And Sydney Clair noticed her parents stiffen in their chairs.

Grandmother turned to Mr. Wilcox. "Are you sure that's a good idea?"

"We want Sydney Clair to make her own friends," said Mr. Wilcox.

"And Patrice is a very sweet girl," Mrs. Wilcox chimed in.

Grandmother shook her head. "That wouldn't happen in my day. Colored folk were meant to be hired hands—not friends to go get ice cream with. Is it even safe for her? Have you read the news lately?" Grandmother was now waving her napkin in the air. Sydney Clair had never seen her so upset.

"We're not in Jackson or some of the places that are more dangerous. And the Civil Rights Act that President Johnson passed last year gave Negroes the right to share the same employment and social privileges as us. So they should have a right to be friends with Sydney Clair, too. Don't you think?"

Grandmother shook her head. "It's just not meant to be that way."

The rest of dinner felt quiet and awkward. And for the first time Sydney Clair could remember, she was glad to see Grandmother leave.

As she watched Grandmother trudge away from the porch, her dad called for her and her mother. "Let's have some family Bible reading time tonight," he suggested. Occasionally the family would gather, Dad would read a certain passage, and they would talk about it.

Sydney Clair sat cross-legged in front of her dad's worn recliner, her chin resting in her hands. She'd known her grandmother to be right about a lot of things. After all, she could beat anyone at Scrabble. If Grandmother had a problem with colored people, then was there really something wrong with them? Was there something wrong with Patrice?

"Why does Grandmother think I shouldn't be friends with Patrice?"

Her parents looked at each other before her mother spoke. "Grandmother grew up in a time of segregation."

Sydney Clair narrowed her eyes. "What does that mean?"

"It means Negroes and white people didn't mix," Dad said. "But things are changing in our country, and colored people are getting more rights. It's just taking a while for society to get used to it. People like your grandmother are used to things being the way they've been for a long time. Change is hard."

Sydney Clair nodded. She kind of understood. She didn't like the change of Penny going to college. Her room had been too quiet last night without Penny's steady, sleepy breathing.

Mr. Wilcox opened his weathered Bible and started to read. "This is out of John 3." He cleared his throat and read about Jesus' conversation with Nicodemus. He ended with, "For God so loved the world, that he gave his only begotten Son, that whosoever believeth in him should not perish, but have everlasting life."

Mr. Wilcox looked up from his Bible. "Some people back in Jesus' time didn't believe everyone should receive everlasting life. But the Bible says that God so loved the *world*—not just white people or colored people or nice people or whoever, but the whole world."

"And so he gave Jesus to *all* of us. To people of every race and every color and every background. Jesus died for everyone," Mrs. Wilcox added.

Sydney Clair nodded. "And if God loves everyone, no matter what color they are, we should probably love everyone, too. Right?"

Her mother smiled at her. "I think that's absolutely right."

CHAPTER 3

Shopping

Sydney Clair loved the smell of department stores like Woolworth's and Sears, Roebuck, and Company. Her mother bought most of her clothes through the catalog, so it was a special treat to go downtown. Perfume wafted from the cosmetic counters as she and her mother opened the doors to the department store. Mrs. Wilcox quickly directed Sydney Clair to the clothing section. Sydney Clair still needed to get a few items for school—maybe a new dress for Vicky's birthday party.

Her mother held up a shift dress with bright green flowers on it. "What do you think?"

"I like it. What about this skirt?" Sydney Clair pointed to a nearby rack of clothes.

Mrs. Wilcox shook her head. "They're making skirts so short these days."

"Penny has one like it."

"Your sister is in college. She buys her own clothes," Mrs. Wilcox said.

"What about this?" Sydney Clair held up a psychedelic print blouse. "Look at all the colors in this!"

Mother appeared disinterested. "I think I'd get a headache if I looked at you too long." She smiled wryly.

But Sydney Clair hardly heard her. She'd just seen the most perfect dress. A mannequin posed proudly in a yellow coat dress with a matching brimmed hat. "Oh, Mother! Look!"

"Now that is fancy," Mother said with a smile. "It would be lovely with white gloves and tights."

Sydney Clair's eyes danced with excitement. "May we get it? It would be perfect for Vicky's party."

Mother examined the daisy detail on the dress, then the price tag. She looked at Sydney Clair, whose breath was suspended in anticipation. "I suppose we can buy it," she said.

Sydney Clair wrapped her arms around her mother's waist. "Oh, Mother. You're wonderful! Wait 'til Dad sees me!"

After selecting a couple more dresses for school, they found some wide ribbons for Sydney Clair's hair and then moved on to the shoe department.

Mrs. Wilcox pointed out some new patent leather shoes. "You're outgrowing your old ones," she said. She picked them up and looked at the price tag. "Four dollars. They get more expensive every year."

Sydney Clair loved the look and smell of new shoes. She paraded down the aisle in them as her mother watched.

"Put them back in the box and we'll buy them," her mother said.

Sydney Clair's throat started to feel parched. "May I get a drink of water?"

"Certainly," Mrs. Wilcox said. "I'll purchase your things and then meet you by the water fountain."

Sydney Clair skipped over to the fountain. An older gentleman was using the larger water fountain, so she leaned over to drink from the smaller one.

"That one's for colored folk, dearie," the man said, stopping her mid-slurp.

Sydney Clair straightened up. What did the man mean? Was she not allowed to use this water fountain? She looked up at the man, who continued to peer disapprovingly over his eyeglasses at her. She filed in line behind him and got her drink.

Her mother appeared soon after with the bags, and the words tumbled out of Sydney Clair as she told her mother what happened. "I didn't know what to do."

Mrs. Wilcox gave her a hug. "Some people still live in the past," she said. "Not too many years ago, there were signs over water fountains saying 'white' or 'colored.' But those signs were outlawed, and now anyone can use whatever water fountain they want."

"Then why do people pretend the signs are still there?"

"Some people aren't ready for change."

"Like Grandmother?"

Mother nodded. "Like Grandmother."

"At least now we're all using the same water fountains," said Sydney Clair. "Most of us are anyway."

"Austin isn't as bad as some other places in the South, but we still have our problems. Like even though Negroes have the right to vote, they're still discouraged from doing so. Some places require that they take voter registration tests with questions like 'How many bubbles are in a glass of water?'"

"Who would know the answers to those kinds of questions?"

"That's exactly the point. Whites would make up those questions to make sure the colored people failed the test.

Some of the Negroes gave up trying. So even though they're allowed to vote, they don't."

Sydney Clair was beginning to see the problem. "Those people need to be stopped."

"And they will be. President Johnson recently signed a law that forbids those kinds of practices. So now many Negroes are encouraging other Negroes to sign up to vote. But it's a long process. People are scared. In other areas, houses are set on fire or people are beat up for trying to register to vote."

"Wow," Sydney Clair shook her head. "I can't imagine that."

"In fact, Mrs. Jackson—Patrice's mother—is in a group that's signing people up next week. They're planning to stage a march to get the attention of colored people in the community and to set up a place for them to register. And it's also their way of saying to the white people who oppose them, 'See, you can't stop us!'"

"She must be pretty brave. Mrs. Jackson, I mean," said Sydney Clair.

"She is. I respect her a great deal," Mother said.

Sydney Clair thought that was another way that she and Patrice were alike: they both had really good mothers.

She noticed Mother had stopped to scribble something down on a piece of paper. "What are you writing?" she asked.

"Oh, I'm jotting down this phone number for your dad. That store is hiring a new manager," Mother replied. She tucked the number into her purse and continued walking.

"Why do you want Dad to get a new job?" asked Sydney Clair.

"Your dad works hard—too hard sometimes. And I think he could do really well in a more professional career. It would be less physically demanding than the factory, and it would pay better."

Sydney Clair remembered how her dad would come home with stories of the jokes he and his fellow workers at the factory played on each other. He'd always laugh his deep, strong laugh as he relived the day's prank. "But Dad seems happy doing what he's doing," she said.

"And I think he could be even happier doing something else," said Mother.

By now they'd reached the bus stop, and Sydney Clair collapsed on the bench.

Mrs. Wilcox glanced at her watch. "Would you like to go visit your sister?" she asked.

Sydney Clair clapped her hands. *Would* she? Of course!

"If we take the bus down to the campus now, we'll still make it back in time for dinner," her mother said.

"Can we take her out for ice cream?" asked Sydney Clair.

"I think she'd love that."

♡ ♡ ♡

It was a hot bus ride to the University of Texas campus. Sydney Clair was eager for the cooler months to come. It was never cold for long in Texas, but when the cold days came, they were icy cold. The Austin climate seemed to teeter-totter between the frigidness of winter and the sweltering heat of summer. The bus door hissed open, and Sydney Clair and her mother disembarked.

"We'll need to walk from here to Penny's dorm," said her mother.

Even though Sydney Clair was hot, the thought of seeing her sister gave her renewed energy. It had only been a few days since they'd dropped her off at school, but it felt like she had so much to tell her. She wanted to talk to her about her new friend, Patrice, and what Grandmother had said. And how she wanted to make curtains to put in the playhouse. And how Vicky was going to have pony rides at her birthday party. And how her Sunday school teacher got a new hairdo that looked like a bee's hive.

Her mother's voice broke into her thoughts. "Looks like there's another protest going on here."

About sixty students carried poster boards with peace signs on them. A number of them were chanting, "Give peace a chance! Give peace a chance!"

Sydney Clair wondered if anyone ever studied or went to class at college. It seemed all they did was wear flowers in their hair and yell things. She wondered if Penny was as uncomfortable as she was with all this ruckus. Poor Penny. She had to live with it every day—including her weird roommate, Moonbeam. It must be driving her crazy.

"Mother! Sydney Clair!" a voice called out of the colorful clump of students.

Sydney Clair looked around. It sounded like Penny.

"Over here!" Penny emerged from the crowd, holding a white flower and her own painted sign. "Be part of the solution, not the problem!" it read.

Sydney Clair could tell Penny had borrowed clothes from Moonbeam's closet. She wore a wild paisley-print top and a bright-colored headband in her now-straight hair. What happened to Penny's pretty waves?

"Your hair. It's straight," Sydney Clair said.

Penny laughed. "Yeah, I ironed it. Pretty cool, huh?"

Sydney Clair hated it.

Mrs. Wilcox spoke up. "Sydney Clair and I were hoping to take you out for ice cream."

Penny looked back at the crowd of people chanting behind her. "That's so groovy of you, but I've got to stay with my people."

Sydney Clair's face fell. They just rode all that way on a hot bus to visit Penny, and she didn't want to spend time with them?

"What are you protesting?" asked Mrs. Wilcox.

 "The war. The government is sending soldiers over to Vietnam to kill people. They need to be stopped," Penny explained.

"What good is this doing?" asked Sydney Clair.

"It's something. It's making our voice heard. Eventually, the establishment has to listen. The newspaper was here earlier. Some of the group actually went out to California to stand in front of trains that were carrying soldiers."

Sydney Clair couldn't believe it. Stand in front of trains? "That's dangerous!"

"The trains will stop. That's the whole point."

"What's happening, babe?" A young man who looked vaguely familiar to Sydney Clair came up behind Penny.

"Tommy, this is my mother and sister," said Penny. "Mother, Sydney Clair, this is Tommy."

Tommy gave them a nod. "Peace."

Sydney Clair realized where she recognized him from. This was the guy who'd been leading the protest when they dropped Penny off at college. The guy with long hair. Up close, she could see he wore round glasses on his scruffy face.

"Hello, Tommy," said Mrs. Wilcox. "It's nice to meet you."

Sydney Clair was quite certain it wasn't nice to meet him, but she bit her lip to keep herself from saying so.

"Right on," said Tommy with a nod, and then he turned

to Penny. "Doll, we're heading over to rap at the student center. The press might be there with some questions. I'm hoping to give them a quote."

"That's far out, Tommy. I'll be there in a minute."

Tommy sauntered off. Penny grinned as she watched him leave. "Isn't he one cool cat? We've been kinda seeing each other. I really dig him."

Sydney Clair hardly understood what Penny was saying. "You should come with us. You don't need to be around them; they're going to get you in trouble."

Penny rolled her eyes. "I'm not a J.D., Sydney Clair. I need to say what I feel. I need to be a part of this. This is bigger than ice cream."

Sydney Clair felt like she'd been slapped. "What's a J.D.?"

"Short for juvenile delinquent."

"You're acting juvenile. . . ." She couldn't remember the second word Penny had used. "You're probably that other word, too."

Penny shrugged. "Mellow out, little Daisy. It was groovy of you to make the trip down here, but you should've let me know ahead of time. I'm doing my thing now."

Mrs. Wilcox nodded. "We'll see you some other time then."

"Yeah, that'd be out-of-sight," said Penny. "I need to go." She tucked the daisy she'd been holding behind Sydney Clair's ear. And with a half-wave, she turned around and walked off.

That was it? That was their visit? Sydney Clair thought. *And Daisy? What happened to Clair-Bear?*

"Why didn't you make her come with us, Mother?" she asked.

Mrs. Wilcox guided Sydney Clair back to the bus stop. "She's in college now—an adult. I really can't make her do anything. She makes her own decisions."

Sydney Clair felt her eyes well with tears. She felt hurt . . . and angry. How could Penny just brush them off like that?

"I don't like college. They dress funny and . . . and I don't like that guy Tommy." She brushed a tear off her cheek.

Mrs. Wilcox gave Sydney Clair a kiss on the top of her head. "I know, honey."

"Why is she being like this?"

"The world is going through a lot of changes right now," said Mrs. Wilcox. "It's exciting and a little scary."

Too many changes, Sydney Clair thought, as she sat on the bench waiting for the bus. There seemed to be an awful lot going on in the world—a lot she didn't understand. She was glad that she got to stay home with her parents and play with her friends in her playhouse. She snuggled in close to her mother, who put her arm around her and gave her a hug.

"Sydney Clair," her mother said, "sometimes the world seems to be in chaos, and I don't know what to do about it. But the one thing I do know is that God is still in control. And I trust him. I pray for you and Penny every day. And I know God is big enough to take care of you even when I can't."

After dinner that night, Sydney Clair sat at the table in her playhouse. She could see a full moon hanging in the night sky outside the window. She still felt angry toward Penny. The visit had been so disappointing.

Bo snuck in through the open door and rubbed against Sydney Clair's leg before resting his head

on her lap. Sydney Clair scratched the dog behind his ears and looked out the window again. She noticed all the stars— hundreds of them. It reminded her of what her mother said earlier: "God is still in control."

Sydney Clair closed her eyes and whispered a prayer. "God, I know you're in control of the universe, and Mother and Dad always say you care about me even more than you care about the stars in the sky. So I wanted to tell you how I feel right now. I'm worried about my sister. Please help her not to change too much." She paused. "And help me not to miss her so much. It really hurts. Amen."

She opened her eyes, and suddenly one star seemed particularly brighter.

"Do you see that, boy?" she asked Bo. But Bo had his eyes closed, enjoying having his head scratched.

"It's twinkling for me." Sydney Clair felt in her heart that God was sending her a message that he indeed was in control, and he'd heard her prayer.

"Thanks, God," she whispered.

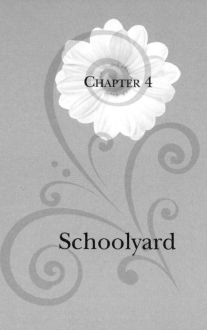

CHAPTER 4

Schoolyard

"I can't wait for you to see the dress Mother bought me for my party," Vicky said. "It's lavender with a poofy skirt and a lace collar. It's so beautiful!"

Popcorn spilled to the ground as the girls giggled and talked about Vicky's party and the first day of school. It wasn't like Mrs. Wilcox to agree to a sleepover the night before school started, but when Ann's mother called and asked Mrs. Wilcox if she'd watch Ann so she could care for her father, Mother put her own preference aside. Vicky was a bonus. Sydney Clair had assured Mother that it was only right since they were all three best friends.

"I can't believe the party is coming up this Saturday," Sydney Clair squealed.

Ann picked up her doll, making it dance to the music playing on Sydney Clair's record player.

Vicky's doll joined in.

Mother arrived at the doorway, twisting and turning to the music.

"Oh, Mother!" Sydney Clair declared, burying her head in her pillow.

"I just stopped by to tell you ten more minutes then lights out. Remember it is a school day tomorrow. I'll be back to tuck you girls in and hear your prayers." She danced away from the doorway.

On the walk to school the following morning Sydney Clair had a skip in her step. She was in the same class as her two best friends. She liked school. She liked the smell of new pencils. She liked having lunch with her friends. And she especially liked all the books. She admired her new lacy socks and walked faster. School was only a couple blocks away, and she couldn't wait to get there.

"We're already going to be early, speedy," Ann said. "You can slow down."

"I know. I'm just excited!" Sydney Clair said.

"I'm so glad we have Mrs. McMannis. Everyone says she's the nicest teacher in the fourth grade," said Vicky.

Fourth grade! Sydney Clair felt so grown up walking to school with her friends. They passed the bakery and the barber shop, waving a quick hello to Mr. Benson, who was giving an elderly man a shave.

The brick school building came into view, its American flag waving proudly out front. Sydney Clair grabbed and squeezed Vicky's and Ann's hands. She was sure this would be the best school year ever.

The shrill school bell rang to announce lunch. Sydney Clair quickly stuck her reader and pencil in her desk and met Ann and Vicky at the door.

"Did you hear Laura has a new doll? I want to play with it when we go outside," Vicky said.

After lunch the girls situated themselves on the grass under a big oak tree out in the schoolyard. Vicky talked more about her party on Saturday.

"My dad will be making the hamburgers, but everything else will be bought at the deli," she said proudly.

Sydney Clair heard a shy voice overhead. "Hi, Sydney Clair."

She looked up and saw Patrice. Her shiny, black hair was back in a plaid headband that matched her jumper.

"Patrice!" Sydney Clair jumped up and gave her friend a hug. "These are my friends, Vicky and Ann."

"Hi," said Patrice.

The other girls mumbled hello.

"I didn't know you were going to this school," said Sydney Clair.

"We moved into this district with the new house. It's my first year here. I'm in fifth grade."

"Who do you have as a teacher?"

"Mrs. Plum."

Sydney Clair nodded. "I hear she's really hard."

"I don't know yet. It's only the first day," said Patrice. "But she reminds me of Miss Beadle."

Sydney Clair giggled, remembering the teacher in the Little House on the Prairie books.

Patrice held up a jump rope. "Some of us are playing over by the jungle gyms if you want to join us."

Sydney Clair nodded. "Sure." She turned to Vicky and Ann. "Come on. Let's go."

"Uh. . . ." Vicky wadded up a piece of trash in her hand. "I told Laura I'd come see her doll." She got up and walked away.

"And I think I want to find a game of dodge ball somewhere," said Ann. "I'll see you later."

Sydney Clair watched them go, feeling confused. She, Vicky, and Ann had always played together at recess. They'd been best friends for years. It was strange that they would just walk off and do something else. She'd have to ask them about it on the way home. But for now at least she could play with Patrice.

"So what do you think of the school?" asked Sydney Clair, as she and Patrice headed over toward the jungle gym.

Patrice shrugged. "Everything you have here is new— books, desks, playground equipment."

"New? We've had the swing sets for years."

"Well, they seem new to me. You should've seen my other school," said Patrice.

"What was it like?" Sydney Clair had never considered that other schools might be different from hers.

"We didn't have enough desks and had to share. Some of them were falling apart. The roof leaked, so on rainy days we had to keep buckets on the floor. And the books were all really old. We got them used. It was a colored kids' school, so no one cared much about it."

"That doesn't seem fair," Sydney Clair said.

"I'm glad we at least had a school."

"So do you like it here?" Sydney Clair asked.

"I miss my friends. There's only one other Negro girl in my class, and you can tell some people don't want us here."

They approached two girls jumping rope, and Patrice introduced them. "Sydney Clair, this is Ruby and Lena. Ruby's in my class, and Lena is her little sister. She's in third grade."

Ruby, Lena, and Patrice knew all sorts of jump roping chants that Sydney Clair had never heard before:

Old Number 12

Comin' down the track.

See that black smoke.

See that old engineer.

Tol' that fireman,

Ring that bell.

Well, well, well,

Jesus tell the man.

Say, I got your life

In my hand, in my hand.

Sydney Clair was having fun learning the new songs when she noticed a crowd of kids from her class approaching. They made their way toward Sydney Clair and stood in a half-circle around her. *What's going on?* Sydney Clair wondered. Vicky stood in front with her arms folded over her chest, staring hard at Sydney Clair. Patrice stopped jumping, and the rope fell limp to the ground.

"Sydney Clair," said Vicky. "There are a group of us that are going to play games on the *other* side of the playground. You can join us if you'd like, but these girls aren't invited." She pointed to Patrice, Ruby, and Lena.

Why would Vicky say such a thing? But looking in the faces of her white classmates, Sydney Clair began to understand. They didn't think she should be playing with these girls.

These were the people her mother had talked about—the people who thought they were better than colored folk. They were people who thought Negroes shouldn't be treated the same way as whites.

"So, are you coming?" asked Mona, a red-haired girl in Sydney Clair's class.

Sydney Clair felt like her words were stuck in her throat. She didn't know what to say.

She looked from face to face of the children gathered around her. Many of these kids she'd known since kindergarten. They'd done plays and variety shows together and gone on field trips. Johnny, Trina, Mona, Karen, Martin, David, Lucy, and, of course, Vicky and Ann.

Vicky stood with her arms still folded, tapping her foot on the dusty ground, waiting for Sydney Clair's response.

Sydney Clair looked at her friends. She dressed like them. Their parents were friends. She had the same skin color. Did that mean they were supposed to hang out together? Her grandmother had said as much. Maybe she was right. But then Sydney Clair thought about what her parents had said. Wasn't the right thing to treat everyone equally?

Ann walked up to Sydney Clair and whispered so no one else could hear, "Sydney Clair, if you play with these girls, no one else is going to play with you anymore."

Sydney Clair glanced behind her at Patrice, Ruby, and Lena. They stood silent, with the whites of their eyes wide and stark against their dark faces. She knew they were excluded at school. They weren't surrounded by friends. They wouldn't get picked for teams in gym class. They wouldn't be invited to birthday parties. They'd be left alone most of the time. Sydney Clair didn't want that for herself.

She clenched her fists. She didn't want to be treated like they were treated. She wanted to be able to get ice cream when she wanted it. She wanted to be liked and accepted. But she also wanted Patrice as a friend. Sydney Clair felt like a ping-pong ball was bouncing back and forth in her brain.

Ann continued, "It's for the best. White kids are supposed to play with white kids, and colored kids are supposed to play together. It's the right thing for everyone. You're doing her a favor."

Sydney Clair took a deep breath, her decision made. She walked over to the group of her white friends.

"Let's go play," she said.

Sydney Clair didn't know what expression Patrice wore when she walked away. She didn't dare look back to see.

Sydney Clair fiddled with the peas on her plate that night, mindlessly balancing them on her fork.

"You seem pretty quiet tonight, Sydney Clair," her dad said. "Especially for the first day of school."

"Yes," Mrs. Wilcox agreed. "Did you girls stay up too late? I shouldn't have let you have a sleepover." Mrs. Wilcox shook her head disapprovingly.

Mr. Wilcox patted Mrs. Wilcox's hand. "Dear, you helped a friend." He looked back at Sydney Clair. "Tell us about your teacher. Do you like her?"

"She's nice." Sydney Clair swallowed.

"And did your friends have good summers?" asked Mrs. Wilcox.

"I think so." She reached for her milk and took a big gulp. "May I please be excused now?"

She was anxious to be out of her parents' sight. She thought for sure they could see into her brain and know what she had done that day. They'd know that she'd abandoned Patrice because of her color. That she'd joined forces with all the white kids. It was the very thing her parents opposed, and now she was guilty. She was the prejudiced one. Certainly her mother would find out tomorrow. Surely Mrs. Jackson would tell her at work.

"You haven't even had dessert yet," her dad said.

"Are you feeling all right?" Her mother placed a cool hand on her forehead. "You don't feel warm."

The doorbell rang, and Mr. Wilcox jumped up to get it. Sydney Clair breathed a sigh of relief, happy to be out of the spotlight.

"That's odd. It's late for someone to be coming by," noted Mrs. Wilcox.

From the dining room, Sydney Clair could see a uniformed police officer standing at the door.

"Gerald!" Mr. Wilcox said. "Is there anything wrong?"

"Sorry to bother you, Frank, but I have some news for you. It's about Penny."

Mrs. Wilcox quickly wiped her mouth on a napkin and rushed into the living room. "What happened?"

"She's fine, ma'am. But we did have to take her down to the station. She and some other students at the university were blocking the Marine recruiting office today, scaring people from signing up."

"She was arrested?" said Mr. Wilcox.

"Oh, no. Nothing like that. It was peaceful enough. But

we do have her down at the station. You'll need to come down and sign some papers."

"Let me grab my coat," Mr. Wilcox said.

♡ ♡ ♡

Sydney Clair laid in bed that night unable to sleep. Surely the heaviness she felt in her chest would have to go away sometime. But it didn't. It seemed to weigh heavier than ever. She thought of Patrice watching her leave their game to go play with the other white kids. She thought of her sister at the police station. Today had been easily marked as a "bad day" in bold, black letters.

She wondered if Patrice's calendar said the same thing.

Sydney Clair heard the front door creak and knew her dad must be home. Maybe he'd brought Penny with him. She hopped out from under the covers and padded downstairs.

Mr. Wilcox stood pouring milk into a pan on the stove.

"Is Penny here?" Sydney Clair asked.

Her dad turned, surprised to see she was still up. He shook his head. "I took her back to her dormitory. Were you waiting up for her?"

"No, I just couldn't sleep."

"Do you want to have some warm milk with me?"

Sydney Clair nodded and sat down at the table.

"Did they have Penny in handcuffs at the prison?" she asked.

Her dad chuckled and set a steaming mug in front of Sydney Clair. "She was at the police station, not the prison. And they didn't have her locked up at all. I think the police just wanted to scare her by taking her in."

Sydney Clair felt some relief. She'd been picturing Penny sitting in the corner of a cold cell eating stale bread with her ankles shackled. "So was she scared?"

"A little bit I reckon." Mr. Wilcox sat down across from his daughter and took a sip from his own mug of milk. "Not as scared as I was when I got taken in to the police station."

Sydney Clair's jaw dropped. *Her dad had been arrested?*

Mr. Wilcox smiled at Sydney Clair's unveiled shock. "Yes, your dad has been in trouble once or twice."

"What did you do?"

"This was a few years back. You were just a young thing," her dad said. "There was a group of colored men staging a sit-in at a soda shop downtown, and—"

"What's a sit-in?" asked Sydney Clair.

"Well, there was a time when colored people weren't served at restaurants and the like. So, as a form of protest, some of them would sit at lunch counters. Not fight or anything . . . just sit," explained Dad.

"Did they ever get any food?" Sydney Clair asked.

"Nope. And some people would get really mad that they were there. They'd pour ketchup and salt and water on them. But those colored folks—they just sat there. Making their point without saying a word."

Sydney Clair was confused. "So why did *you* get arrested?"

Mr. Wilcox leaned back in his chair, remembering. "Well, the police eventually showed up and dragged them out of the soda shop. They were hitting the colored kids with billy clubs, and it just didn't seem fair. So I jumped in to help the Negroes, and they took me down to the station, too."

"Wow." Sydney Clair felt the heaviness return to her chest. "So you were just helping them."

"Tried to. Didn't do much good," Mr. Wilcox said.

"Does that kind of stuff ever work?" She wondered about all the marches and signs she'd seen down at the college. Mrs. Jackson's rally. The marches in Montgomery. Did it really make a difference?

"Slowly," he said. "A lot of brave people who chose to put themselves in situations opened themselves up to harassment and persecution and it finally made a difference. People had to take notice, and things eventually started to change."

"You really care about that stuff, don't you?" Sydney Clair said. "All the equal rights and everything."

"I really do. Your mother and I both do," he said, then paused for a bit. "It's hard sometimes, though. My own mother believes in segregation, so she disapproves very strongly when I want to support racial equality."

Sydney Clair felt a knot form in her throat. "It must be tough to do something Grandmother doesn't like."

Dad nodded. "It's never easy swimming against the flow. But sometimes we just need to decide to do what's right— and trust that God will take care of the rest."

If Dad knew what I did to Patrice, he'd be so disappointed in me, thought Sydney Clair. *I haven't been a friend. He went to jail for what was right, and I couldn't even jump rope on the playground.* She faked a yawn. "You're right. I'm tired. I should get to bed. Goodnight, Dad."

CHAPTER 5

The March

"If we mix together these donkey noses and add in some ancient Egyptian salts, the mixture will be perfect," said Ann.

Sydney Clair watched Ann stir pine cones and table salt together. She wondered what Ann was concocting in the playhouse today. But she also had other things on her mind.

"Did it seem like Vicky was avoiding me today?" Sydney Clair asked.

"She's been distracted with her big party. And she came in late because of her dentist appointment," said Ann.

"It seemed like she was avoiding me. She hardly said anything to me today," said Sydney Clair.

It had been strange not to walk to school with Vicky. She wanted to tell Vicky about the gloves she was thinking of wearing with her new yellow dress for the party. Was it possible that Vicky was still upset with her about yesterday, even after the fun sleepover? She'd chosen Vicky over Patrice—what more did Vicky want?

Ann glanced out the playhouse window. "Well, you won't have to wait long to find out. She's coming toward us now."

Vicky usually bounded up to the playhouse full of news and ideas. But today her demeanor was far more distant.

"You're just in time," said Sydney Clair. "Ann is making. . . ." She really didn't know what Ann was making, so she ended with, ". . . something frightening."

"I really can't stay," said Vicky. "I only came over to tell you, Sydney Clair, that . . ." Vicky hesitated and stared down at her feet. "I don't think you should come to my party on Saturday."

"What? Why?" said Sydney Clair.

"Well, you know how my father is on the city council?"

"Of course," said Sydney Clair. Vicky's mother mentioned the fact every chance she got.

"Well, he heard from the police chief about your sister getting arrested and—"

"Your sister got arrested?!" Ann broke in.

"She didn't get arrested!" Sydney Clair noticed her voice going up an octave and stopped to take a breath and calm herself. "She only got taken down to the police station."

"Wow! What did she do?" asked Ann.

"Nothing. It was silly," Sydney Clair said.

"Well," Vicky said, "my mother is concerned about what people will think. And she said it would probably be better for all of us if you don't come."

Sydney Clair couldn't believe what she was hearing.

Vicky continued. "Mother says that we've worked hard to establish a good reputation in the city, and with Father on the city council we really need to be careful about who we associate with." She cast a sad look at Sydney Clair. "I'm sorry. It's what Mother said."

Sydney Clair shook her head. She felt like she'd been punched in the stomach. This didn't seem possible. She was one of Vicky's best friends. She'd been planning on going to this party for months. How could she be uninvited because of something her sister did?

"You're right, it's not fair," Mrs. Wilcox said, wiping her hands on her apron. "But it's Vicky's party and her decision. There's really nothing we can do about it."

"It sounded like it was more her mother's decision," muttered Sydney Clair.

"Mrs. Taylor does care a great deal about upholding her family's reputation," said Mrs. Wilcox.

"Can we go over on the day of the party and stage a sit-in?" Sydney Clair pictured herself carrying a sign in front of the Taylor driveway that instead of stating, "Give peace a chance," said, "Give Sydney Clair a chance."

Her mother smiled sadly. "I don't think that would be a good idea."

Sydney Clair crossed her arms over her chest. "Well, I'm certainly not going to give her the doll I bought for her."

"That's your decision," Mother said.

Sydney Clair felt like her mother didn't care nearly enough. Shouldn't she go over there and tell the Taylors what she thought of them? Shouldn't she fight for Sydney Clair to be re-invited to the party? She knew these were ridiculous thoughts. As her mother had already said, it was Vicky's decision. Sydney Clair couldn't make anyone invite her to their party. It was just hard to sit and do nothing—to watch such an injustice be ignored.

"It wasn't even something I did that bothered them. It was all Penny—Penny and her strange friends."

"I know." Mrs. Wilcox stuck the pan of bread in the oven and sat down at the kitchen table. "And I don't want to minimize how hurtful this is to you. I know you and Vicky are good friends, and it stings when a good friend betrays you."

Sydney Clair thought of Patrice. Maybe this was God punishing her for being mean to Patrice, making Sydney Clair feel the same way she had made Patrice feel—like an outcast.

Sydney Clair wondered if Mrs. Jackson had told her mother what had happened. "Did Mrs. Jackson talk to you today?"

Her mother looked away. "Yes she did. Why do you ask?"

"Just wondered." Sydney Clair shrugged. She braced herself for the bad news.

Mother's words fell slowly. "She asked me to help register Negro voters on Saturday."

Sydney Clair was confused; her mother appeared troubled. "What's the matter?"

Mother sighed. "Sometimes it is hard to do the right thing."

Sydney Clair leapt for joy on the inside. If Mother found it difficult to do the right thing, then maybe she wasn't so bad after all. "Well, what are you going to do?"

Untying her apron, Mrs. Wilcox said in a determined voice, "Colored people live with unjust treatment every day of their lives. They're thought of as less and are given fewer privileges simply because of their skin color. That is not fair at all, is it? There's nothing wrong with the color of their skin. It's just different than other people's."

Sydney Clair shook her head. It certainly wasn't fair. Why did the colored people's school have to use old books? Why did Henry not give them ice cream? Why did people like her have to be so mean to them?

♡ ♡ ♡

At school the following day, Ann called, "Your turn," as she finished skipping over the chalk-drawn hopscotch board.

Sydney Clair barely noticed. She was looking across the playground, hoping to see Patrice. She knew she needed to talk to her.

"Are you looking for Vicky?" asked Ann.

Sydney Clair shook her head. Vicky was still giving her the cold shoulder.

"Are you mad that I'm going to the party Saturday?" asked Ann.

"No. You should go. It'll be fun. I'll find something else to do."

Just then she saw Patrice with her friends. The three colored girls were playing near a grove of trees, their dark legs peeking out from plaid jumpers.

"I need to go talk to someone," said Sydney Clair. "I'll see you later."

Patrice, Ruby, and Lena saw Sydney Clair coming and huddled together. They stopped whispering as Sydney Clair got closer and simply watched her.

"Hi, Patrice," said Sydney Clair.

"Hi." The girls crowded closer together.

"I just wanted to tell you . . . I'm sorry about the other day."

"What's there to be sorry about?" said Patrice. "You were just being who you are."

"What do you mean?" Sydney Clair asked.

"It means you're white, and because you're white you don't like people like me."

"That's not true! I do like you. I want to be your friend!"

Patrice's mouth set in a tight line. "Well, you sure didn't act like it the other day."

"I know. I said I was sorry."

"So you want to be a friend that plays with us when no one else is around. Then when your white friends come by, you just leave us like old rags. No thanks. I don't need any friends like that."

"That's not the kind of friend I want to be—" Sydney Clair faltered. She didn't know what else to say. Patrice's eyes were spitting fire.

"Words don't mean much. You didn't act like a friend. And that's way more important than saying you're going to be a friend."

Sydney Clair looked down at the ground and dug the toe of her shoe into the soft dirt. She knew Patrice was right. She knew she hadn't acted like a friend, and why should Patrice trust that anything had changed? She wasn't even sure she wouldn't hurt Patrice again. She knew she didn't want to, but . . . well, that didn't mean much.

The other girls walked off and, this time, Sydney Clair was the one left all alone.

Saturday morning Sydney Clair awoke from a fitful night's sleep, went downstairs, and tearfully told her mother everything that had happened. Mrs. Wilcox handed Sydney Clair a tissue, and Sydney Clair wiped her eyes. Sitting at the kitchen table, she felt better after talking about what had happened on the playground, but she still felt ashamed. And now she'd lost two friends, Vicky *and* Patrice. With Penny becoming a different person, it felt to Sydney Clair like her whole world was falling apart.

"I'm glad you told me," said Mother.

"I'm sorry I didn't tell you earlier. I knew you'd be disappointed with me. You and Dad both. And God. I really messed up."

"It's hard to stand up against the pressure of your friends and classmates," said her mother.

"But what you said yesterday is true," said Sydney Clair. "My feelings were hurt because I was treated unfairly by Vicky on one occasion. I can't imagine having to deal with that every day like Patrice does. And then *I* became one of those people who mistreated her." She blew her nose. "I feel awful."

"Do you remember us talking about the verse in John the other night?"

"Of course. Everyone knows that verse," Sydney Clair said. She recited John 3:16 in her head: *For God so loved the world, that he gave his only begotten Son, that whosoever believeth in him should not perish, but have everlasting life.* "We talked about how God gave the gift of Jesus to everyone."

"That's right," her mother said. "But did you do anything to earn that gift?"

Sydney Clair shook her head. She knew she must've disappointed God. She wondered what Mother was getting at. She felt badly enough already.

Her mother gave her a soft smile. "God gave us that gift because he is good—not because we are. That kind of gift is called grace. It is not something we earn."

Sydney Clair's brow wrinkled. She was confused.

As if she could see into Sydney Clair's mind and read her questions, Mother asked, "What about people who do bad things?"

"Yes," Sydney Clair said. "If God gives grace and it is not because we obey—" She stopped.

"Then why be good? Why obey?" Mother asked.

Sydney Clair nodded.

Mother softly cupped Sydney Clair's chin. "Why do you obey your dad and me?"

Sydney Clair's blue eyes fixed on her mother's as she spoke softly. "Because I love you . . . and I know you love me." At those words, Sydney Clair realized she had answered her own question: *Because I love God and I know he loves me is why I obey him.* She thought for a moment. That meant God loved her—even with all her mistakes—because he was good, not because she was. And if God loved her like that, Sydney Clair wanted to love others like that.

"Mother, I've got an idea," she blurted. Pushing back from the table, she jumped to her feet and scurried from the room.

Within minutes she reappeared wearing her new yellow coat dress and hat.

"Honey, you can't go to Vicky's party, no matter how badly you want to."

"I've got a better idea," Sydney Clair announced.

The bus door hissed open, and Sydney Clair watched as a large crowd of people filed down the bus aisle. She'd never seen so many colored people in her life. For once, she was the minority. She not only stood out with her white skin, but also in her fancy yellow dress. She could feel people staring at her. Her mother must have sensed her nervousness because she squeezed Sydney Clair's hand.

"We're doing the right thing," Mrs. Wilcox whispered in her ear.

Sydney Clair nodded. She stood up, clutching a sign with her sweaty palm. They exited the bus into a huge swarm of Negroes. She felt lost in the midst of the crowd and held tighter to her mother's hand.

"Hold up your sign!" Mother shouted to Sydney Clair over the roars and chants of the crowd.

Sydney Clair held it up. "Register to vote. It's your right!"

The rally was starting to attract more people by the minute. Hundreds of colored people stood in line to register. A couple people looked at Sydney Clair and her mother strangely, as only a handful of white faces stood out in the crowd.

"You want me to vote, little girl?" An elderly Negro man peered down at Sydney Clair.

"I do," said Sydney Clair. "You should register."

The old man shook his head. "Well, I'll be. This little white girl wants a colored man to vote. Lord, what's next?"

Sydney Clair had to smile as the man got into line.

The crowd started swaying and singing a gospel song. And Sydney Clair swayed right along with them, even though she didn't know the words. But then they started singing a song she recognized. Of course, it was one Ruby and Lena had sung the day they jumped rope. Sydney Clair added her voice to the chorus.

Mrs. Wilcox pointed toward some tables that were set up with voter registration forms spread over them. "There's Mrs. Jackson."

Sydney Clair recognized the colorful kerchief on her head and her bright smile.

"Let's head over there and say hello," her mother said.

The two maneuvered their way through the crowd like fish swimming upstream. It wasn't until they got to the table that Sydney Clair saw Patrice sitting next to her mother. She froze momentarily. What if Patrice was still mad at her?

Mrs. Jackson gave Mrs. Wilcox a hug. "I'm so glad you're here!" she kept saying. Patrice sat stiffly in her metal folding chair and eyed Sydney Clair suspiciously.

"It was Sydney Clair's idea," said Mrs. Wilcox.

"Bless you, child." The colored woman wrapped Sydney Clair in a warm hug.

Patrice looked up. "It was really your idea?" she asked.

Sydney Clair nodded. "After I treated you so badly on the playground, someone treated me unfairly, too. And it made me realize how much I hurt you. I really like having you as a friend, and I don't ever want to hurt you again. I want to show you that I feel you should be treated fairly. You and all colored people. That's why I'm here."

Patrice mumbled, "Even if it means losing your friends?"

"Yes," Sydney Clair said. She was going to be gracious whether people deserved it or not.

Patrice waved to Sydney Clair motioning her toward the street. "Then let's march!"

"You're on!"

♡ ♡ ♡

The two girls headed toward Congress Avenue, making their way toward the Capitol. Sydney Clair remembered Dr. Martin Luther King Jr.'s words: *I have a dream that one day little black boys and black girls will be able to join hands with little white boys and white girls as sisters and brothers.*

"Maybe tomorrow you can come over and play in my playhouse," said Sydney Clair.

"You don't think your friends will mind?"

"It doesn't matter what they think. I want you there."

"Maybe we could pretend that we're friends of Laura Ingalls Wilder and we're waiting for Almanzo to get back," said Patrice.

"Yes! We could pretend that it's blizzarding out and we are all running out of food," added Sydney Clair.

"My name will be Dianna," Patrice added.

Looking at Patrice's big smile and their mothers laughing, Sydney Clair thought maybe change wasn't so bad. She flashed her own big smile. "My name will be Daisy. It fits me—y'know, who I *really* am. I bloom where I'm planted."

Patrice gave Sydney Clair a quick hug. "I'm going to mark this on my calendar as a 'good day' for sure."

Sydney Clair smiled back. "A *very* good day."

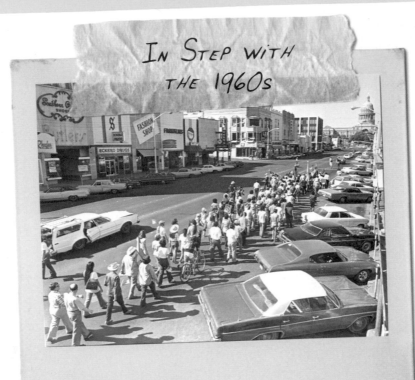

IN STEP WITH
the 1960s

Protesting

During the 1960s young people in America grew disillusioned with the ideals of previous generations. Society became a battleground where the status quo was confronted. Protestors were as varied as their many causes: the civil rights movement, anti-Vietnam movement, women's rights movement, environmental movement, and more. Traditional values were no longer accepted merely for tradition's sake. Values had to be proven on the stage of human lives.

Protest march down Congress Avenue in Austin, Texas in the 1960s.

Austin History Center, Austin Public Library

PRESIDENTIAL FAITH IN GOD

Presidential Faith in God

The United States was devastated on November 22, 1963 when its beloved president, John Fitzgerald Kennedy, was assassinated. In that moment of terrible violence, America's sense that promises could be fulfilled by its leadership was shattered.

It was as if Kennedy himself warned against this false belief in his inaugural address: "The world is very different now. For man holds in his mortal hands the power to abolish all forms of human poverty and all forms of human life. And yet the same revolutionary belief for which our forebears fought is still at issue around the globe, the belief that the rights of man come not from the generosity of the state but from the hand of God. . . ."

The main campus and tower on
the University of Texas campus
in the 1960s.

Education that Recognizes an Almighty God
Many people, academic institutions, and government offices acknowledged the presence and leadership of Almighty God, as testified by the biblical inscription on the landmark tower on the University of Texas campus: "Ye shall know the truth and the truth shall make you free." (John 8:32)

Culture

In the 1960s slang was the communication of teenagers.

Dictionary:

Bread: *noun*—Money. "How much bread is it going to cost you?" (Also dough, loot.)

Bug: *noun*—A small foreign car such as the Volkswagen, not including sports cars. "For a bug that size, it uses a lot of gas."

Clyde: *noun*—A person one insults or dislikes; a clumsy person. "You clyde! When will you ever grow up?"

Coconut: *noun*—Someone who acts as if he were of low intelligence. "You're acting like a coconut. Sit still in the pew."

Fuzz: *noun*—A policeman, policemen. "The car thief was picked up by the fuzz." (Also skinner, cop.)

Groovy: *adjective*—Great, wonderful, good. "That's a groovy jacket you've got." (Also boss, tuff.)

J.D.: *noun*—Abbreviation for juvenile delinquent. "I wish he didn't act like a J.D." (Also judie, hood.)

Juvey: *noun*—Juvenile hall. "Then they hauled me to juvey."

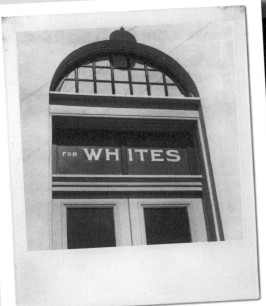

18527 Austin History Center, Austin Public Library
(NOV. 1949 Stuer S.A. TEX.)

Civil Rights
America in the 1960s was not sublime for everyone. Countless Americans were struggling hard to obtain their basic human rights in the 1960s. Many businesses, including service stations and restaurants, would not do business with African American people. Some businesses went so far as to remove the stools at their lunch counter so African Americans would have no place to sit.

AS-60-27281-9 Austin History Center, Austin Public Library

Even though the Austin Public Central Library was desegregated in the 1950s, it still showed signs of racial discrimination by the all-white staff. The only exception was one African American janitor.

28253 Austin History Center, Austin Public Library

Sydney Clair's
public library

15751 Austin History Center, Austin Public Library

Going away party in 1966 at the
Austin Public Library
for janitor Andrew Bragger.

AD-60-272-60-1 Austin History Center, Austin Public Library

Civil rights protestors picketing Woolworth department store in Austin, Texas

Civil Rights Movement

Many Americans stood against racial injustice by marching, participating in sit-ins, picketing establishments, and even resorting to violence. Martin Luther

King Jr. became a figurehead of the civil rights movement as one of the most visible advocates of nonviolence as a method for social change. This student of theology was *Time* magazine's Man of the Year in 1963 and the recipient of the Nobel Peace Prize in 1964. Persecuted yet persistent, Martin Luther King Jr. gave his life for his conviction that it is God's desire that all of mankind should have freedom.

Girls 'n Grace COLLECTIONS

We celebrate the strength and wisdom that we have in Christ, so today and into the future we can become all that God has purposed. ❀

Girls 'n Grace 18" dolls have been beautifully sculpted by the renowned doll artist Dianna Effner.

International characters!

Discover an international community of Girls 'n Grace from Africa, the United Kingdom, India, Peru, and more!

I Can Through Christ!®

Girls 'n Grace Like Me! Collection

❀ Choose a doll that looks like you!

Sydney Clair: A Girl 'n Grace in the 1960s

When industrious Sydney Clair Wilcox finds herself lonely in the summer of 1965, she determines to do something about it. With her best friends, Vicky and Ann, Sydney Clair sets off on an enterprise to make money to purchase her heart's desire: a fun-loving golden retriever. Join Sydney Clair as she finds for herself mishaps, merriment, and meaning.

Mesi: A Girl 'n Grace in Africa

Mesi (pronounced *Maycee*) is a girl growing up on the continent of Africa. The landscape is as diverse as its people and their beliefs. Mesi's education and her family's well-being are threatened by drought, disease, and war. Yet, amidst these hardships, Mesi discovers a God who is near, so near that he cares about what concerns her. Along her journey she finds out about his inexhaustible treasure called grace.

Order online
www.GirlsnGrace.com

I Can Through Christ!®

Girls 'n Grace NIV New Testament

With an attractive cover to attract this generation of reader, Girls 'n Grace offers an NIV New Testament, the most widely accepted contemporary Bible translation today. The NIV New Testament was created to accurately and faithfully translate the original Greek, Hebrew, and Aramaic biblical texts into clearly understandable English.